A CALL FOR JUSTICE

ANKITA BANERJEE

ISBN 979-888521782-8

Chapter -1

"Eventually all things fall into place. Until then, laugh at the confusion, live for the moments, and know everything happens for a reason"

-Albert Schweitzer

I came across this quote just a few minutes ago. Turns out Albert Schweitzer was right indeed-taking me for example, I had no plan of writing anything today but here, I am, wondering about what to write.

The first thought that comes to my mind every time I think of writing something is an autobiography. I mean, not a serious one, not about the life-altering events that one experiences in his lifetime. Quite frankly, I don't have many of those. And having said that I don't mean to imply that my personality has not developed over the years. It's just that my ways of being self-aware are not entirely conventional. I like to perceive the world in a different light that is mostly foreign to others.

And personally, I feel more inclined towards stories that reveal the brighter side of life, that have happiness wrapped around itself, that have hope for a better future, and happy memories that are not overlooked and overshadowed by the inevitable dejection that follows thereafter. I feel that shunning those moments robs us of our own happiness.

I for one, live for the brief moments of exultation. It gives me a sense of purpose, something to wait for and to keep moving forward.

The incident that I am about to write is one that inspires hope and belief, that there is always a better ending waiting for us and all we have to do is be patient enough to get to it.

Before I begin with the story it'll be convenient to give a brief background about myself. I'm the younger daughter of my family. I grew up in different places due to my father's transferable job.

I had always been a little disconnected from my family and more connected to books. Over the years, my penchant for books and solitude had been so persistent that my family found it in the best interest of everyone to send me off to study abroad. As a result, by common accord, I was sent here, to Chicago for higher studies.

Although my sister hadn't been particularly keen on the idea of me being here completely by myself but eventually, she acquiesced. My mother, on the other hand always seemed to have an unascertained belief that I am organized enough to live by myself.

And it was her faith in me that made me believe in myself furthermore.

So, I came here, to Chicago. I live with my roommate Ayesha. I was enamored with her from the very first day of college. I remember the day I met her quite vividly. It was Genetics class and I was sitting on the fourth bench, attentively listening to the professor's stultifying and endless lecture about the origin of life. It had been raining incessantly that morning.

Suddenly a knock on the door startled everyone. It was a girl completely drenched, trying to get hold of an umbrella, a bag soaked in water, some soggy books, and a cell phone all at once. Her pitiable condition was reason enough for the professor to let her attend the class that day albeit she was 40 mins late to it.

Noticeably discomfited, she walked in and chose to sit beside me.

After settling in quite comfortably, she said with a sheepish grin, "Hi, I am Ayesha."

"And this is Ruhani," I replied with a smile.

That was our first encounter. It may sound a little cliched but I felt an instant connection with her. I don't quite know how but I found an unvarnished genuineness in her. We gradually became friends over the next few days. Eventually, we rented an apartment together and became roommates as well. It all happened so fast that I could hardly remember being in the college hostel, which was where I was originally supposed to spend my college days.

I am glad I didn't have to. The mere thought of those boisterous girls, gossiping about boys day and night makes me nauseatic.

Although Ayesha wasn't entirely immune to those sorts of things, we had a mutual understanding of not including me in those discourses. And that somehow strengthened our friendship even more.

Chapter – 2

Now, coming to the day of the incident, a day that started on a mundane basis but ended up being the day I can never obliterate from my memory.

That day we had the last examination of our second semester. Everyone was in high spirits- happy and excited about the semester break that was about to commence from the next day.

Some of my classmates arranged a party that night, the sort of party I don't usually go to. I'm not being conceited but there's nothing that can lure me to those parties and even if somehow, I bump into one, I find myself hiding in a corner, enjoying my solitude with some appetizers and mocktails in hand.

I have never been a social butterfly. My friend Ayesha on the other hand loves to hang out with friends and tries abortively to include me every time she goes out.

That day was no exception. After a series of unyielding arguments, she gave in and finally left for the party at around eight.

I locked the door from inside and went to the bathroom to have a quick shower. After a refreshing bath, I decided to have some leftover pizza from the other night and spend the rest of the night watching a movie. After all, having some alone time is a pleasure I seldom encounter, so I tend to seize any chance I get every now and then.

As soon as I opened my laptop to get started with my plans for the night, my phone rang. I glanced at the name on the screen. It was Ayesha. I picked it up.

"Hey, are you okay?" she asked anxiously.

"Never been better, why do you ask?"

"I don't know, I just tried calling you a few minutes ago to inform you that I might be late today and a girl picked up and said hello. I thought it was a wrong number, so, I hung up and redialled. But again, the same girl picked up. And this time she told me to ask you to call her immediately."

At this point, I interjected- "who? Me?"

Ayesha continued, "yes, you. And the craziest part is she knows your name! I was so creeped out that I hung up right away."

At first, I thought it must be some practical joke that Ayesha must be pulling on me for abandoning her tonight, but her voice suggested otherwise.

"Are you sure this is not a joke?" I asked dubiously.

"I know how much you hate this kind of joke, trust me, I'm really worried about you", she said gravely.

"There must be some mistake, I think you are drunk and imagining things."

I don't know why I said that as I clearly knew from her voice that she wasn't drunk at all. Perhaps I was comforting myself.

"You're a douche!" she said irkly.

"Come on, enjoy your party. I am fine here." I said, trying to sound coherent.

"Okay, but take care."

She hung up the phone.

I thrust my phone on the bed and continued to rummage through my collection of movies on the laptop. But I couldn't concentrate as the conversation with Ayesha kept playing in my head over and over again. Something about it felt amiss. My mind was burning with curiosity.

Finally, I gave in to the temptation of calling that girl myself. Quite impetuously, I took my phone and dialed my own number. As I did so, it felt ridiculous at first but then a strange, inexplicable shiver of fear riveted my attention. Little did I know that it was only the beginning of a reckless venture.

Chapter - 3

After three beeps, it started ringing. I felt an icy shiver of fear as soon as I realized that someone has picked up on the other side.

"Hello, Ruhani. I'm..."

I felt my heart thudding in my chest. I was unable to speak and hung up but only to call her again. But this time I waited for her to complete her sentence.

"Hello, Ruhani. Please don't hang up on me. I just want to talk to you. Would you please hear me out?"

I tried to contain the dread I was feeling but failed miserably.

"How do you know my name? who are you? What do you want?", I asked with a quavering voice.

"I will answer all your questions, just hear me out for once", she implored.

I couldn't deny that I was not curious enough to know what was actually going on. So, I acquiesced.

She continued, "I'm Riddhima from Akash Nagar. We used to live in the same neighborhood about 10 years ago, do you remember? We used to play together; we were great friends back then. She paused, earnestly waiting for a response.

A vague picture of us playing in the backyard of my childhood home got clearer as she spoke. Riddhima, yes, she was one of my closest friends back when we used to live in Akash Nagar. We lived in the same neighborhood. We even went to the same school for 5 years. We were practically inseparable.

"Yes. Yes... of course, I remember you! How are you? It's been so long!"

"10 years! It's been 10 years. I'm glad you remember me. I thought you must have forgotten me or something."

"How can I forget you?" I said, abashed at the thought that I never called her after we left Kolkata.

"Actually, after my father got transferred to Delhi, and I really got caught up in there, new home, new school... everything was so different. I had lost contact with almost all of my friends. But I'm glad that you called", I said eagerly.

"There's nothing more exciting than reconciling with an old friend."

"Absolutely" I exclaimed.

But how did you get my number and how come your number is the same as mine?"

"Oh! that I did with a new app. You should try it. It's quite fun! And I got your number from your Facebook account. You must have forgotten to hide it from the info section "

"Have I? Honestly, I don't remember " I replied vaguely.

"I must apologize for calling you like this but I had no option. You are my only hope.", she said anxiously.

"What is the matter? Are you okay?"

"Actually, I ran away from my house last night. I couldn't stay there for another day!" she said dolorously.

"Is everything okay? Where are you now?"

"Don't worry about me. I'm in a safe place. I'll tell you all about it later", she assured.

"Sure, whenever you're comfortable".

I was taken aback for a moment. I never thought of Riddhima as a person who'd bolt off from her home. I was wondering what made her take such a rebellious decision?

"So, as I was saying, I'm in a devil of a mess right now.

Would you do me a favor? It'd mean a lot to me"

"Of course, what's the matter?", I queried.

"All you need to do is go to my house and deliver a tape recorder to an address mentioned on its back. I forgot to take it with me yesterday. It's on the right shelf in my room and the key is under the bed."

"Are you sure everything's okay?", I asked again.

"It's a long story but I'm fine as for now. Would you mind doing me this favor?"

"But don't you think your parents will know you have contacted me if I go there?", I asked tentatively.

"They will not understand. Trust me. Please do this for me. I would never ask for anything else ever! Promise!"

She spoke in a quavering voice. I never imagined that she is capable of pleading with someone for help. She was so brave and courageous even as a child. She was the one who got me out of trouble every time something bad happened. And as I was engulfed in thinking all this, I realized that I felt deep compassion for her. All of a sudden, I knew that I should help her. And anyway, it's unlikely for anyone to call up an old friend out of the blue only to ask for help until and unless he or she is in a grave problem. And as far as I knew her, she was always the one who helped others and seldom the one who needed it herself. So, I was sure there was definitely something wrong and that I should help her, at least for old times' sake. So, I said:

"Okay... I'll do it... But what's in that tape recorder?"

"You'll get to know everything eventually."

She said pensively.

And then again continued:

"Thank you Ruhani. I knew you were the only one whom I could trust! Thank you so much for everything."

"It's absolutely fine. But I wanted to ask you something--- hello? Hello, Riddhima are you there?"

The call ended abruptly.

I remained silent for a moment, processing all the information in my head. The whole thing seemed preposterous. I started mulling things over and soon my head filled with hundreds of questions.

Had she called me to genuinely ask for help or there's more to it than I am yet to comprehend? What if this is a trap or some kind of a joke? And most importantly what is in the tape recorder, why is it such a big deal for her?

I knew there was only one way to get all my doubts clear. I must find-

I dozed off.

Chapter - 4

"Hey, wake up you sleepyhead! Don't you have a flight to catch?", a faint voice woke me up.

"what's the time?" I queried.

"It's almost ten", Ayesha yelled from the kitchen.

"What? Why didn't you wake me up? I have to be at the airport by 11", I screamed.

"This is my third attempt to wake you up dumbo! And besides, I came home late last night. I woke up just half an hour ago", she said languidly.

I dropped the conversation and got myself ready within fifteen minutes and left for the airport in a cab.

I was forced upon by my family to spend the semester break with them, at home, in India. I complied with the idea in order to avoid the perilous situation that would have taken place otherwise.

My mother had said, "It would do me good to come home for some time."

Now I have one more reason to do so; Funny how things lined up in perfect order without causing any inconvenience, I thought to myself on my way to the airport.

At around, I landed at Dum Dum airport. It took me two hours to finally reach home from the airport.

As I set foot in my home, I discovered that my mother had arranged everything I needed to sleep off my weariness for that day. And I did accordingly.

The next morning I woke up to a text from an unknown number stating:

"I called you yesterday but your phone was off. Please send me a text as soon as you are done with the job. I'm waiting to hear from you very soon."

The text felt more like an order than a request. But by then, I had already made up my mind to help her and so I decided to ignore the tone of the text.

"Finally, you're awake, Ruhi", my mother said while entering the room.

"Breakfast is ready, come down. It's been so long that we have had a proper conversation", she said with great gusto.

"Coming, mom. Just a second", I replied with a smile.

At the breakfast table, I asked mom about Riddhima.

Just as she heard the name, her face turned pale.

"Yes, I can recall her. It's a pity what happened to their------"

My mother was interrupted by the sound of the doorbell that pealed through the house.

It was our housemaid, Leela. She is a nice woman but an inveterate talker. She appeared impetuously in the doorway, then stopped and peered at me inquisitively.

"How are you beta?", she asked.

"I'm fine. Thanks", I replied briskly.

There was a pause. I knew it was my only chance to get away from there. So, I said:

"Mom, I need to go someplace. I will be back in an hour."

Chapter – 5

It took me a while to reach the place. I couldn't recognize the house at first. It was not how I remembered it. There used to be a huge palm tree in the backyard where we played every day. It wasn't there anymore. The house seemed somewhat dull and lifeless. The sun seemed to cast aside his warm light from the house. As a result, it was enveloped in cavernous darkness and a pall of gloom.

As I approached the house, a picture of Riddhima and me playing on the stairs rose clearly before my mind. I reflected for a minute or two, staring wistfully at the mansion. I couldn't bring myself to ring the doorbell.

I had not thought of any excuse as to why I was thereafter so many years. I wasn't even sure if anyone's in the house.

"Are you looking for someone?", a voice startled me from behind.

As I turned around, I discovered it was Sidhu kaka, the caretaker of the mansion.

"Sidhu kaka!", I exclaimed.

"I'm sorry dear, do I know you?", he replied cordially.

"Sidhu kaka, it's me, your candy thief — ruhani, riddhima's friend"

"Oh! Ruhani beta. Sorry, I didn't recognize you. You have grown so much! The last time I saw you, you were just a little girl."

"It's been 10 years kaka", I said.

There was a momentary silence. Then he spoke again.

"How are you Ruhani beta? How is Mr. and Mrs. Sen?"

"We are all doing good. I came to India yesterday for my semester break. I'm doing my higher studies in Chicago."

"Very good dear, you were a great kid. I always knew you were gonna do good in life."

I smiled.

Then, he asked:

"But what brings you here beta?"

"Riddhima!" I exclaimed. "She called me a few days ago to help her out with something. I'm quite worried about her situation. How is her family, Sidhu kaka? They must be worried sick. Is there anyone in the house right now?"

I said it all in one breath.

And at once I saw the repulsion, the horror, in his face. He stared at me as though I were a ghost.

"Sidhu kaka? Are you okay?"- I asked impatiently.

"Ruhani beta, what are you talking about?", he paused for a moment and then again continued:

"Riddhima died in an accident four years ago. She was found dead inside her bathroom. Her parents moved away after that, and the house has been empty since then."

Everything fell silent for a moment.

I felt like passing out. I tried to remain rooted to my spot but it became harder every passing second. I couldn't make sense of anything that happened for the past few days. Was it all in my head? Have I gone completely insane? How is it even possible? I spoke to her that day over the phone and the text! Yes, the text that she sent me today, that cannot be unreal.

I rummaged through my bag to find my cell. As I took it out, I discovered that it's dead. But I remembered charging it just a few hours ago. The conclusion that I was being driven at was too incredible.

"Are you okay? Do you want me to bring some water, dear?", Sidhu kaka inquired.

His voice brought me back to my senses. I stood there utterly stupefied as Sidhu kaka brought me a bottle of water. I splashed some of it on my face and drank the remaining.

"Do you feel a little better?"

"Yes, kaka. Thank you."

"You wait here, I am calling you a cab. You should go home and rest for a bit."

My mind was somewhere else. I felt a strangely irresistible enticement towards the house. I couldn't battle out the temptation and finally gave in as I made up my mind to go inside the mansion.

"I want to go inside", I blurted out.

"What? Have you gone insane?"

"I have this feeling, I can't explain it to you but I know I have to go inside, I was told to do that. There ought to be some explanation behind all this."

"The house has been empty for three years and after all that happened in here, I cannot let you inside the house. This place is not safe anymore Ruhani beta."

"I just want to check something. It wouldn't take long. I know you have the keys to the house. They must have given you a spare one. Would you please do me this one favor?" I said obstinately.

There was a pause.

"I cannot do that. It is risky."

"I'm not going anywhere until you give me the keys", I said fractiously.

He sighed and then spoke again.

"You must know the risk involved in letting you in there?"

"I know kaka, but I also know that if I don't do what she told me to, I'd never be able to forgive myself. She was one of the closest friends I have ever had. I can't let down our friendship even when I know she'll never get the chance to get offended anymore."

It seemed that something I said resonated with him.

"Okay, if you insist so much, I assume there must be some valid reason behind it", he said reluctantly.

"Thank you so much. I knew you would understand me."

He handed me the keys and said,

"10 mins. You promise me you'd be back within 10 mins."

"I promise."

Sidhu kaka saw me depart with visible reluctance.

Chapter - 6

As I entered the hallway, I had a queer feeling of being watched, spied upon by something unearthly. I was unnerved by the deathly silence that filled the whole mansion. There was a pervading sense of discomfort and strangeness that suffused the house. I didn't feel remotely safe being there in the middle of a horror house. But something told me to go on with the expedition and so I continued.

I mounted to the bedroom of Riddhima. I didn't recognize it at first. Everything was different than what I remembered.

The bedroom stank of filth. The table, the window, everything was thick with grime.

I strode towards the bed immediately, as if I were under a spell or something. I looked under the bed and found a key. I took it and proceeded towards the shelf.

There was a sudden hiss and roar as I saw the rain come down through the window.

I flung opened the door of the shelves and at once a tape recorder fell down with a resounding crash. I picked it up and noticed the address of the local police station taped at the backside of it.

"Hurry up Ruhani beta, it's raining outside, you should get home as soon as you can", I heard Sidhu kaka's voice from the porch. I hurried downstairs and after thanking him again, I took a cab back home. As soon as I reached home, I briefed the mysterious events to my mom.

"We got some vague information about an accident involving her family a few years ago. But I had no clue about Riddhima", she said dolorously while I stared at her.

The whole thing was a muddle that I was yet to comprehend. But quite ironically, after that morning, very few thoughts passed through my head, the most eminent of which was the disembodied voice that spoke to me over the phone a few days ago. The gravity of the situation and something indefinable that tinged it reduced me to silence.

My mother believed the incredible events that I witnessed for the last couple of days. She advised me to do exactly what I was told to and so I did.

I went to drop the tape recorder at the local police station the next morning.

As soon as I entered the police station, I noticed the swift gleam of surprise which showed in the inspector's eyes, before the professional reserve came down his face once more. He knew me since I was ten years old. I used to go there as a kid with my father who continues to be a great friend of his even now.

I plunged into a careful narrative, embodying all the facts that I encountered for the past couple of days. After a lapse of a minute or two, I noticed profound skepticism and a trace of suspicion on the inspector's countenance.

I was forced to explain in detail-a long, tedious explanation which included everything that happened.

The inspector heard me to the end.

"Are you sure, this isn't some kind of a prank or something?", he said at last.

"I'm pretty sure it's not."

There was a trace of hesitation in his manner, as though he found the story quite hard to stomach. But eventually, he acquiesced.

I handed him the tape recorder and he agreed to look over the matter as soon as he can.

I left the police station with the moral satisfaction of knowing that I had done everything I was instructed to. It didn't bother me much, not knowing what was inside the tape recorder. I was pretty satisfied with the role designated to me in the entire plot. I decided not to jinx it by questioning the course of action that followed.

Chapter – 7

Three months had elapsed when I finally got a call from the police station. The inspector informed me that the parents of Riddhima have been arrested in charge of murder against their own daughter. A thorough inquest was done on the basis of Riddhima's confession in the tape recorder, cross-checking every statement that was recorded by her just a few days before she died. However, the reason behind this atrocious murder is yet to be known and further investigation is expected to shed some light on it.

For a moment I was dumbfounded. There was something ruthless in the merciless analysis of the affair that struck fear into me and for a minute or two I remained silent.

I think I can safely say that I had imagined almost every possible occurrence that could lead to the same out-turn and so the truth when it came, was subconsciously expected.

Nevertheless, I wasn't fully immune to the horror that it struck me with but somehow managed to accord with the circumstances.

Everything got back to normal from there on like nothing ever happened. It seemed as if the whole thing was meticulously planned by someone who contemplated every move that was made and dematerialized once the intent was accomplished.

We were just a tool in the process of achieving something bigger, something that seemed insoluble to mortal abilities and needed the assistance of some unearthly specters.

I have always been skeptical about supernatural and paranormal activities. They never made any sense to me. But I reckon that the things that we are yet to comprehend don't negate their inevitable existence.

I never heard from Riddhima after that, neither did I try to dial my own number again.

Contents

Acknowledgements

I wish to express my gratitude to the site of notionexpress for giving me the opportunity to publish my first ever story. Thanks to my parents and my sister whose love and support made this possible in the first pace. I'm extremely grateful to my friend Banshita for supporting me throughout the process of writing.

Above all, to the creator of knowleadge, humanity and wisdom, for his immense love, thank you.

Ankita Banerjee

www.ingramcontent.com/pod-product-compliance
Lightning Source LLC
Chambersburg PA
CBHW020657160726
47991CB00003B/1229